Standing
on my
head

Also by Hugh Prather

How to Live in the World and Still Be Happy

Love is Letting Go of Fear

The Little Book of Letting Go

Love and Courage

Notes to Myself

*Spiritual Notes to Myself: Essential Wisdom
for the 21st Century*

*I Will Never Leave You: How Couples Can Achieve
the Power of Lasting Love*

Standing on my head

Life Lessons in Contradictions

Hugh Prather

CONARI PRESS

This edition first published in 2004 by Conari Press,
an imprint of Red Wheel/Weiser, LLC
York Beach, ME
With offices at:
368 Congress Street
Boston, MA 02210
www.redwheelweiser.com

Library of Congress Cataloging-in-Publication Data
Prather, Hugh.
    Standing on my head : life lessons in contradictions / Hugh
Prather.
        p. cm.
    ISBN 1-57324-918-1
    1. Conduct of life. I. Title.
    BF637.C5P82 2004
        158.1—dc22   2003017998

Typeset in Berkeley Oldstyle

Printed in the United States
RRD

11 10 09 08 07 06 05 04
 8 7 6 5 4 3 2 1

A Word about Words

I didn't sit down to write this book. It evolved from a notebook in which I recorded thoughts, problems, insights, difficulties—a practice I have found helpful much of my life. The entries I have selected are in chronological order, at least in terms of internal time. Taken as a whole I believe they exhibit a curious pattern: Every time I think I have learned something, my life seems to deliberately set about contradicting it. Yet the contradiction is never absolute. It is more a quarter turn than a whole. So I have left the contradictions side by side, because that's the way life is.

There are probably no absolute answers. Just alternatives. The best I can do is to trust my present experience and follow where it leads. And it has led me down some amazingly divergent paths, from Mary Baker Eddy to Fritz Perls, from Krishnamurti to *A Course in Miracles* ... but somehow, at the time, each one worked, each one was needed, and, conversely, each became a cage when I clung to mere words in spite of my experience. This mistake was never the fault of the particular teaching. Once again, I had unplugged myself from my core.

So I want to remind you that every entry in this book is at best an asymptotic shot at life, and at my life, not at yours. If my words affirm you, then savor them for the moment. But if they tempt you to distrust your basic honesty, spit them out. We are the only authority on what is good for us. Once we see this, we feel an enormous peace and freedom.

soft the sky
fills
and softly
spills
soft the drop
drips
gently down
and soft my foot
falls
soft the ground
and down the ground
fills
gently down

There is a flat way of seeing that most of us live with every day. And there is a spiritual way of seeing that comes suddenly, and when it does that day is rare and beautiful. With this new vision we see the innocence woven through all beings and objects, as though a shaft of light had fallen across treasured possessions in a forgotten closet, and for the time we live with this vision, all things around us are transformed.

I associate this spiritual way of seeing with many causes: with music and poetry, with sunsets and seas, with friends who are friends, with love, and now and then with a book or a passage within a book. These things have at times inspired me to this broader vision, but rarely have I been able to return and use one of them to recapture it. If I try, the poem or song will have lost its magic, and I only receive an echo of my previous wonder.

Sometimes I doubt and sometimes I believe. I like not making myself believe when I am doubting and not making myself doubt when I am believing. Surely neither God nor accident needs *my* consistency.

When I paint I am influenced by the texture of the paper, the viscosity of the paint, the condition of the brush. I reach down to make a thin line and it comes out plump. Then the picture takes a new direction—I influencing it, it influencing me.

We start to do one thing and something happens to divert us. We resent the influence and try to go back to our original intention. But we are *always* influenced because we do not live in a vacuum together with our intentions. We are in a relationship with everything that occurs. We walk down a road and feel a sudden burst of warmth from the sun and stop to bask our eyes. We receive a letter from a loved one, a nibble from our puppy, a knowing look from a clerk in a store and are no longer the same. What we just were doesn't quite apply. What we just intended is in the past. This is not a lack of resolve; it is the way life flows. Always a new painting, always a new self.

Are we more mind than body, more body than feeling, more feeling than memory, more memory than future? Sometimes I am all anger and sometimes all peace. There are minutes I live for tomorrow and minutes I live for her. In last night's hot bed I was flesh and afterward soul. But most moments I am not just a body or a mind, and when I am at peace with this reality, and my intellect does not override my flesh, and here does not deny tomorrow. When emotions, memories, needs and all the *et cetera* of my being each have their own voice, I see that I am how everyone else is . . . and possibly even how *everything* is.

Cause and effect have no stopping point. Everything we do touches everything else. Since I have become more willing to acknowledge my displeasure, I notice that I have started crossing my *T*s. And somehow this is related to the comment I recently made about Beulahs: "She liked me until I crossed her." And all of this appears to accompany my new posture: I no longer hold my head down as much. I suspect there are a thousand other connections.

I do not see growth as a procedure that locates "the real me." It is more a process whereby I become aware of other aspects of myself that are equally as "real" as the familiar me. We are always "being real" to some part of our being and, at that moment, not "being real" to other parts. In this sense we always act— always choose to act—out a particular side of us. There are no such states as "not in touch," "disconnected," or "incongruent." Everyone is in touch with something. There is the state of being *out* of touch— out of touch with areas of the body, with nature, with other people, with less familiar aspects of our personalities. And there is the state of being stuck in what we *are* in touch with. Much of my life I have been aware of my thoughts and little else. And this is true of most of the people I know. They stay pretty much within one chamber of their being.

When Buzz stayed with us I noticed that eighty percent of his conversation was about "Important People I Have Known or Read About." I wonder if most people's conversation centers mainly on a single theme? Dave's appears to be "Interesting Facts About the World Around Us." Beulah's is "Enlightening Experiences I Have Had." Mine is "Insightful Ideas in Psychology."

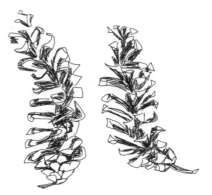

No matter what we talk about, we are talking about ourselves.

My attitude toward much of life is habitual. I have a fairly consistent telephone personality, a different but predictable party personality, and I make about the same kind of grocery store customer every time. I am in approximately the same mood each time I brush my teeth, run an errand, meet somebody, or heat a bowl of soup. I pick out what I am going to wear beginning with my shirt, seldom with my pants, and I shave starting with my chin. I never jump with joy in the shower or act silly while driving. I am mildly good humored when I wake up and never precipitously go to bed. All of these attitudes feel right and veering from them feels phony. I guess it could be said that I am being genuine, but genuinely what?

I feel as if I am slowly dying when my life is in a rut, but my attitude toward ritual is more affirmative. I have a friend whose ritual is popcorn and beer. It begins every evening after his wife goes to bed. He fixes his popcorn to perfection and sits in front of the fireplace. Then his dog lies beside him and receives the first two bites. An elderly relative of mine has the morning ritual of eating breakfast and feeding birds from his large porch while telephoning his friends one by one. My ritual revolves around certain trivial things I do each night before I get into bed, and, for whatever reason, I enjoy going about my preparations in a familiar way.

In order to break with a pattern of behavior, first we have to become aware of how we *usually* act. We have to see how we do it before we can undo it.

At the time, I am not aware of how I shut down my attention or hold back my warmth. When reproached for my lack of feeling, I defend myself because my feelings have been hurt. Usually all that has happened is that someone, usually Gayle, has become more aware of my patterns than I have. This is the gift, not the curse, of a sound relationship.

When going to sleep or waking up, I notice that certain areas of my body feel drowsy while others feel stimulated, and that if I want to sleep I can generally do so by fixing my attention on the drowsy parts. This same principle may also apply to attitudes. When checking to see how I feel about something, I automatically move my attention to the region of my solar plexus. But it appears that there are other aspects of my personality centered in quite different areas of my body. Tonight when I explored these I found that from my back I was strong and stolid, from my feet I felt athletic and slightly impatient, and from my hands I was cool, liquid, and glib. In my neck, eyes, and shoulders there were still other differences. The question, "How do I feel about this?" might be answered, "Feel from where?" In this way I could not deceive myself into believing that I have only one attitude to which I can be true.

I think of the process of "being genuine" as the shuttling of my attention between a feeling and an appearance, between inside and acting out. But being honest or "real" does not mean that I am only allowed to shuttle between my behavior and my strongest emotion. My behavior can match whatever in me I wish it to match. "Being real" is simply being aware of what my actions do in fact match. To believe I must always behave in accordance with my strongest emotion is self-reduction.

At any moment we are free to act from any dimly felt and long-neglected part of ourselves: to be a ham, to be strong, to flirt, to cry, to be totally silly, to dance, or simply to respond from that part of us that recognizes our connection with both the situation and the individuals at hand. If this feels phony because it has been so long since we have chosen to respond from something other than our usual repertoire, still it is not phony. It is part of us; we are doing it. And it is surprisingly liberating.

Humor is a way of relating to people that I feel uncomfortable with. I am more familiar with what it takes to be serious. Seriously.

I am admitting that I want something when I try to be funny. I don't require as much cooperation in order to be serious. Humor comes more easily when I am around people I don't feel I need anything from.

When I try hard to be funny, I am small and gray, but when I am easy with myself, allow other people's fun to sparkle through me, and allow my own lightness to roll gently out, then good humor rhymes in all the sweet times around me.

If I hold back any part of me I suppress that much energy and potential. The question I want to ask myself now is not what behavior is good or bad, but in what ways would I express myself with greater energy if I didn't hold back. I suspect that the qualities I consider ugly are simply ones in which I have not yet allowed my entire force, that if I would express these traits honestly, they might ripen into something full-flavored and whole.

For months I have been fighting my nice-guy game, but today I consciously used it. Gayle and I were sneaking onto the St. John's College tennis courts when two professors drove up. I went over to them, said hello, commented on the wind, asked if they had watched yesterday's U.S. Open final match, and sought their advice on a particular brand of tennis ball. The result was that not only did Gayle and I get to play tennis but also that I felt stronger, more centered, than when I have slipped into this game out of fear. There was something honest about being consciously dishonest: I took responsibility for my actions.

How would I act if I *didn't* feel inept when Dave is being hilarious? How would I write if I *could* write like James Joyce? How would I greet Bob if I *weren't* reserved? How would I look at a woman if I *did* think I was sexy? How would I act if I could act any way I wanted? How would I be if I weren't tired or fat or scared or blocked or whatever it is I am always telling myself?

This morning I let out the long-suppressed Dale Carnegie side of me when I ran into Jim. I had only met him once and really liked him. He lit up at my enthusiastic niceness and invited me to lunch—which is just what I had hoped he would do.

What would I discover about the cottonwoods if
when I walked to the mailbox I listened to them
instead of looked at them? What would I find out
about the rain if I didn't run inside? And is it possible
that a sunrise would refresh me more than sleep?

Tonight at dinner I tried picking up my glass with my
left hand instead of my right and didn't feel quite so
self-assured. It was a nice feeling. It would also be
nice if I didn't analyze everything I did.

Almost every small boy whom I have seen walking down the corridor at the airport runs his hands along the deliciously tiled wall.

There were seventy-five people in the lobby and only a seven-year-old girl was finding out what it felt like to sit on the marble floor.

It's this simple: If we never try anything, we never learn anything. If we never take a risk, we stay where we are. And while we practice constancy, the world evolves around us and we miss so much magnificence.

By holding ourselves back, we trade the opportunity to find out who we are for the illusion of safety.

I say that I accept the way I am, but do I accept it so fully that I am willing to act on it—to actually act the way I am?

I have to act the way I am now before I can become something else.

I agree with Nelson: "We can't change, but we can expand."

This Thanksgiving, Norman said, "I have known you since the third grade. I have seen you as a Christian Scientist, a vegetarian, an avid businessman, and now this, whatever it is. Your ideas change, but you always remain the same."

I am not sure if I have changed either. I know that today I am a little more aware of my body, a little more aware of nature, a little more aware of other people . . . but that's not really "changed." It's more "returned"—returned to some of what I started life with. I also know I am a little more tolerant of the way I am and the way other people are. Those two things usually go together. And I know that I have a few more alternatives now. I am able to respond in some ways that I couldn't a few years ago. I think Norman is probably right—only ideas change. I have read about saints and high people, but I have never known one. Awareness, tolerance, and openness don't seem to change me; they just allow me.

He called tonight. He's going to be a big-time politician, he says. And he probably will. As I listened to him, I thought, "There's a real live human being under all of that."

You say you want "to be somebody"—then apparently you don't want to be yourself.

Fame isn't fame. It only appears that way from a distance.

There is nothing to *achieve*
There *is* nothing to achieve
There is *nothing* to achieve

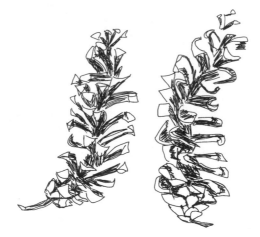

As long as my attention is fixed on future accomplishments, I remain where I am. Ambition has the opposite effect of "getting me ahead." It keeps me stuck. Ambition is an extension of the past. It is a desire for more of something already known or something long desired. *Openness* is what will get me ahead because openness does not know what is ahead—it has no rigid idea of what is needed.

If all the striving, planning, and rehearsing that most of us indulge in actually came true, we would still be left with only a bigger version of ourselves. Real progress can't be imagined. We can't anticipate in thought what new vision life will lay before us or in which direction it will next demand our growth.

All I want is to be able to relax into this moment so I can see what it is offering.

"I wish" assumes that I know what is in true contrast with my present experience.

"You have so much potential." That is a hole yet to be filled. Thought won't fill it. And ambition, which allows only the future to be real, simply makes the hole larger. To stop this clatter in my head I will have to die to the future. I will have to give up "having potential."

So much of what we think of as our worldly identity, when we examine it closely, is just a paper sack filled with leftover desires.

open
and alert
empty
and available
human and
alive

waiting
(without purpose)
ready
(without wanting)
existing
(without needing)

I parked the car in front of the post office and Don and I got out. I got out to go to the post office. Then I realized that Don had gotten out, was walking and noticing, and was only *heading* toward the post office.

Gayle and I took Natasha to meet my parents. When we got out of the car and started toward the door, I was in a state and Gayle was in a state, but Natasha was fascinated with the shrubbery.

Walking without a goal (to get somewhere)
Eating without a goal (to get full)
Looking without a goal (to judge)
Talking without a goal (to convince)
Living without a goal (to accomplish)

There is no harm in wanting to accomplish; the harm is in *having* to accomplish.

My desire to accomplish is as periodic as my desire for food, and when I have it nothing else satisfies me except hard work and a job done with care. But I am not responding to some future picture; I am acting from the present and enjoying the process.

I spend an inordinate amount of time looking for something to *do*, looking for ways to become whole, when all the while my organism, my being, God, or whatever one wants to call it, is making music, and all I need to do is stay with the rhythm.

A problem does not have to be thought about in order to be solved.

Sometimes when I am scared I like to turn on the light.

What *should* I do?

Nothing
Nothing is the thing to do
(Nothing is the only doing)

I am worthwhile just existing
("Just?"—OK, I am worthwhile
existing)

What if the stars were to start doing something?
("What are you doing hummingbird?"
"I'm just being a hummingbird"
"Oh, is *that* all?")

As soon as I start doing
I stop being

"I don't understand how you do so little."
(Now *that's* a compliment)

Not opening a can of tuna because last night's casse-role might spoil if I don't eat it; not changing the ther-mostat because later it might get too hot; or not pulling over the coffee table to eat on because I will have to put it back—I am surprised at how much I indenture myself to the future.

Making our bed, putting up the toothpaste, writing neat lists—my perfectionism centers me in the future.

Whenever I stand up, sit down, start to walk, or start to reach, my attention jumps out of the present and I become temporarily absent from my body. Having a goal, even one so small as getting a glass of water, does not require that I leave my senses. I can know what I want to do and still remain present.

The question is not whether to have goals. The question is whether it's a goal now or a goal then.

Struggling to make her reach a climax is just as much working for a goal as struggling to reach one myself. If I am having sex in *her* future, I am still not having sex now.

Staying with the rhythm of the sanding, watching the wood slide into creamy richness, doing it to be doing it and not just to have it done.

It makes no sense to hurry up—and so mess up—
what I am doing now in order to get started on what I
plan to do next.

Every moment that I am centered in the future, I
suffer a temporary loss of this life. Except maybe
when I was a child, I have probably been alive for
only one or two minutes of every day I have existed.

It's not that "today is the first day of the rest of my
life," but that *now* is all there is of my life.

The paradox of progress is that I grow each time I realize that I can only be where I am.

My growth doesn't seem to be a matter of learning new lessons but of learning the old lessons again and again. Wisdom doesn't change, only the situations.

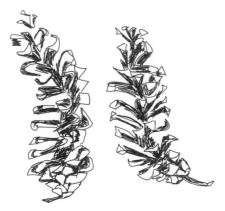

Another kind of "being in touch": being in touch with
the situation and with the people who are here; being
open to the signals that are present. Events and individuals are not controlled by our will. We don't
control anything. It's irrelevant how we *want* things to
be. The question is, how are they now?

Surely this must be an ancient proverb: Never post-
pone happiness by assuming you know what it looks
like.

The black stench of that devastation and the
desperate red flailing and the desire for it not to have
happened. And here I am just taking it in, letting the
dark images fill my mind with fear. Awareness can be
a nightmare, and right now it is too much for me. All
I want is to slowly sink my head into soft boredom
and trivia. I want yesterday.

For the last three weeks I have been comforted by
routine. Sometimes it is necessary to withdraw into
the familiar, to rest in the known until the unknown
becomes less frightening.

Problems don't choose us. "Me against you," and "Me against it" come with having a direction. But *life* is not a single lane. All the lanes are in us. All encounters are crossroads. I think back and realize that so many of my difficulties resulted from staring straight ahead.

Tolerance and intuition are acts of broadening the mind. Grievances and grudges are acts of narrowing it.

How I am working on a problem often indicates how I am keeping it a problem.

So often I wrestle with myself over how I *want* to feel rather than simply observing how I already feel.

I didn't realize until today just how powerful is my fear of being thought stupid. I went into a bookstore and the owner asked me to inscribe some books. As I was writing in one of them I suddenly came to a word I couldn't spell. Ironically, the word was *controlled*. "Does it have one 'l' or two? If I spell it incorrectly they will see it as soon as I leave . . . but if I ask, all these people standing around will . . ." At that point I literally broke out in a sweat.

Attractive women usually scare me, especially tall blondes. I feel slightly inadequate whenever I meet one. If I like her I seem to do everything possible to indicate that I have no interest: I don't look in her eyes unless I have to; I act very innocent and polite; and if her boyfriend or husband is with her, I direct most of my comments to him.

"I feel apprehensive." "Apprehensive" is an interpretation. What I *feel* is a sensation.

This is so important: not to think that I have to do something about the sensations that go off in my body; not to think that I have to give them names and plan immediate action. Instead, to look at sorrow without the word, to look at hunger without the word, to feel what I feel—this time—without forcing connections with the past or projecting future consequences.

I don't have to be sexually aroused *for* something. Simply being aroused can be pure pleasure.

One evening, shortly after I met a famous therapist, I asked her if she would work with me on a chronic stomach problem. She answered that she never worked in the evenings. It had taken a considerable effort for me to ask, and when I heard her words I felt a hot charge move from my chest to my head. Although I haven't always done this before, this time I just stayed with the sensations. I didn't jump from them to thoughts about the therapist. After a few moments the sensations dissolved and the whole matter was finished. There was no hurt still lingering on sentences in my head.

Gayle has just taken in another cat.... to look at cats without the name ... to look at *these* cats without saying the number ... to know what I want to do about this situation, rather than about how it will appear.

To eat an egg without the word. To notice *this:* how it looks, how it tastes, how I feel with it inside me.

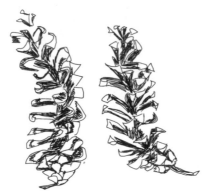

Today I was leaving a small store, weaving my way through the people standing near the door, when the owner suddenly called out, "That's the author!" I immediately went blind with self-consciousness and could see almost nothing until I stumbled out the door. Before the owner spoke, the people I was trying to get through meant nothing to me, but the moment after her announcement they suddenly became important. I was interested in their reactions, but I didn't show it. I just felt intensely looked at. I don't even know if I *was* looked at—I just *felt* looked at. Clearly I only feel looked at by people I am interested in. Probably the feeling of being looked at isn't as strong if we don't hold ourselves back from looking.

Almost any difficulty will move in the face of honesty. When I am honest with myself, I never feel stupid. And when I am honest with myself, I am automatically humble.

Whether it is writing a book, painting a picture, furnishing a room, or cooking a meal, I don't believe that individuals can do it *their* way without being creative.

A lie can sometimes save a great amount of energy— and sometimes so can not telling a lie.

"But you couldn't be sleepy, you had nine hours sleep."

"But you couldn't be hungry, you just finished eating."

"But you couldn't be sick, you just had a checkup."

"But you couldn't be depressed, you just got a new car."

"But you couldn't be bruised, I didn't hit you that hard."

(Dishonesty is a state in which I am mesmerized by words and disregard my experience.)

I am discovering I have kept a few secrets from myself since this incident: I told Dave's son there was a phone in the bedroom if he didn't want to use the one in the living room. He paused a second, then said, "I don't have anything I want to hide."

If I want to talk to someone and I am stuck for something to say, one of the simplest ways to get started is to state honestly what I am experiencing: "I want to talk to you but I haven't a clue what to say." There is also the option of just shutting up.

If I'm rehearsing it, isn't it obvious that I want to do it?

Between desire and action we make our choice for
light or dark, for love or hate, and for peace or chaos.
As long as I am trying to decide, I can't *feel* what I
want to do.

One reason we sometimes have difficulty "deciding"
is that we assume there should be no reservations.
The word itself implies a completion. Often we can
bypass deciding simply by noticing in which direction
we are leaning. Asking, "What is my preference?" cuts
through the perfectionism.

If I do what I prefer rather than what I have
"decided," then I am a little more open to change. I
don't have to think my way back through to a new
conclusion. I simply notice what it is I prefer now.
Of course the larger question is, from what place
within me is the preference coming?

There are many things that I can do a little of at the very moment I find myself thinking, "How awful that I haven't been doing that." I suspect it is no coincidence that my self-criticism comes right at the time I can actually do something about it.

When my day is going poorly, I keep on muttering through it, "until I have time," instead of stopping right then and bringing myself together.

Why is there this fear of pausing, of stillness? Are we afraid of what we will see if we stop long enough to look into our hearts?

By approaching problems with "What might make things a little better?" rather than "What is the solution?" I avoid setting myself up for frustration. I should know by now that I am not going to solve *anything* with one magic stroke—at best I am going to chip away at it.

Problems are never really solved. There is always a residue.

The word *problem* implies an illusion: that this trouble I am having has definable limits—but everything runs into everything else.

I buy things I don't need, then look for ways to use them in order to justify the purchase. In this way I end up doing what I don't want to twice.

Today a friend wrote me, "Do you think you *are* a mistake just because you made one?"

There is no such thing as a mistake. There is only what happened.

Mistakes, like progress, occur in the present. Am I about to side with my baser instincts? Then I am about to make a mistake.

"How much progress have I made?" Meaning, "Am I more tolerant, or more flexible, or more engaged?" Progress is perhaps an unhelpful concept because I am either tolerant this instant or I am not. If I am not, all my "progress" is meaningless.

My day has become a fraction happier ever since I realized that *nothing* is exactly the way I want it to be. This is simply the way life is—and there goes one battle I don't have to fight any more.

Today I heard an elderly woman say, "Whatever I worry about is not worth worrying about."

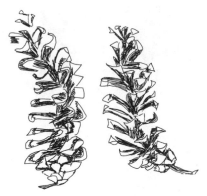

I see that I have made rules for myself about certain words—words such as *why*, *how*, *is*, *feel*, *because*, and *should*. But there are no taboo words, no should or shouldn't words, no rules. It's not words, but what may be happening inside me when I use certain words. All I need is to be alert to what *is* happening, to see where the word is coming from. If I am weighing my words, I am being somebody else. If I don't say what I say, I am an appearance.

I like what Warren McCulloch said: "Don't bite my finger, look where I am pointing."

There are no rules, no shoulds, no
have-tos . . .
I am free.

There are no rules, no shoulds, no
have-tos . . .
I am free.

There are no rules, no shoulds, no
have-tos . . .
I am free.

Growth can get to be such deadly business.

I saw Dina at the party tonight. She smiled brightly and said, "This year I decided to give up suffering."

I am weary of hearing therapists compare therapies. Why this eternal need to debunk? Isn't it obvious by now that just as it is true of any religion, so too, any therapy that makes a person's life happier is good for *that* individual?

A therapy, philosophy, or religion is just one way of seeing. It is an emphasis and as such neglects everything else. A new teaching has at times helped me feel clearer about one or two situations that the old ones didn't, but no teaching has ever seemed to fit my life perfectly. At least I have never found a written statement—esoteric, empirical, or otherwise—that deals *exactly* with something going on in my life right now.

A number of my friends torment themselves over the belief that they can (and therefore should) remove every trace of some block or impasse. These terms, like the expression "work through," imply the existence of the other side ("closure," "duty discharged," or "completed transaction"). I doubt the helpfulness of such a view. What I choose to see as a problem can always be looked at differently. Even among therapies, what one views as someone's "block," another sees as a sign of health. I doubt that it is possible to completely work through such universally held states as anxiety and phobia, although it is clearly possible to move in the direction of greater freedom. I don't even know someone who has *completely* worked through a bitter and chronic resentment, and when I have thought that *I* have done so, a trace of it will surface to remind me that the mind doesn't erase so easily. I am at the place now where if I believe that something in me is disturbing my enjoyment of life, I will work on it for awhile (for as long as working on it seems helpful), but I am losing my zeal for *closure*.

Getting out is getting in
Going in is getting through
(Around is not through)

"I am here" is getting there
"Wish I were there" is staying here
(Moving is standing very still)

Having is getting
Wanting is not receiving
(Being is very filling)

There is still a taboo against having a good time. Somehow life is not supposed to be fun. I have twenty or thirty years left, or maybe it's twenty or thirty minutes, and I believe that enjoying this time may be the *only* thing that really matters.

When I was playing tennis with Nelson this afternoon he said, "As I have been going from one activity to another today, I have been asking myself, 'Is this what I am alive for?'"

Self-discipline ceases to feel like internal warfare whenever I see that, given the alternatives I have allowed myself, I am always doing what I want to do.

There is a kind of trying that affirms me, as when our kitten tries again and again to climb a tree until she has succeeded. And there is a sick kind of trying that denies me, as when I try to make someone like me and become less and less with each failure.

At times it seems that all of my thinking is an effort to become. My thoughts say in effect: "Look at the past, you certainly did that well" (i.e., be more like that in the future), "Look what happened, you sure made a fool of yourself" (don't be like that again), or "Notice what you're experiencing now; here's how you could use it to your advantage" (in the future).

Thoughts are jottings on a memo pad that will never be read.

This afternoon my friend, Ray, looked over what I had written about listening with my eyes to the stars. He said, "Oh I get it, you play the feminine, the yin, and let nature play the masculine, the yang." When you conceptualize it, Ray, you bury it.

As long as I am thinking, I am not fully present.

Jerry told me he was disturbed that his drawings of women always looked sinister. When he added that he often used pictures in *Playboy* to draw from, I said that it was understandable that his drawings looked sinister because these women were acting so phony. Now I wish I hadn't said that. I gave him an explanation. If he accepts it he may now be further away from discovering something about himself than he was before. He wanted to look within himself and I held up a mere explanation for him to look at.

Thinking is a symptom.

That fear generates much of my thinking seems obvious: fear that I might not rise above my past failures, fear that I might not become.

Filling my head with thoughts sometimes gives me the illusion of not being alone.

As soon as I take my attention off my mind, it starts up again. This has been going on for two weeks. I want to clear my mind but it's obvious I can't go about it this way.

(Well, why do you want to clear your mind?
So that I can see the world around me.
OK, then see the world around you.)

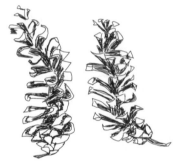

Trying to stop all thinking is like looking into a mirror facing a mirror. My mind splits and confronts itself. To exit the face-off, I have to step into my senses.

The effort to stop all thinking is an army of thoughts warring an army of thoughts. Yet I alone issue the battle cry.

If I attempt to eliminate thinking, I am condemning it. And if I condemn it, how can I see it as anything but bad? The globe of thought is vast, and no one has explored every inch of it

I don't want silence as a rule. I want the *option* of a silent mind.

There are other ways of thinking besides the circular, half-aware prattling that makes up most of the conversations in my head. I sometimes use words to work my way through confusion: to unwind, to untangle. These words create clarity. And there is that state in meditation when occasional thoughts flicker gently in and out of mind like birds on wing or shooting stars. And there is another kind of thought that speaks directly to my core—a sudden seeing with words. Still I am not certain that the words are necessary. I suspect they are not the seeing, only an echo of the seeing. Some day far away, I may be able to put aside all words, like a child puts aside his tracing.

I believe that when my dad wrote this poem, he must have been remembering what it was like to live for a moment without thought:

It was cold and still at night
Stars like lanterns hanging bright
Endless skies with silver tones
Reaching down beyond my mind
Feeling more than what I was
My spirit soaring out beyond
Knowing I could do it now
No matter what the world had said.

Seeing groups of starlit forms
Moving thru some unknown power
Believing I could touch the real
Now that time would pass me by.

Endless worlds were opening up
Colors, forms, unknown before
Chromatic tones of harmony.

Words no longer seemed of use
Old ways of thinking left behind
Images clear as sunlit dew
Flowing freely thru my mind
Being as the image formed
Without space and time between.

Looking back it seemed a dream
Only now was real to me
The depth and feeling of its force
Moving me beyond myself.

One way of looking at a fantasy is to notice what it does for me physically, what it triggers in my body, how it changes my behavior, such as the fantasies I use to get to sleep or the ones I use to become sexually aroused. These may be of some physical benefit. But what of the fantasies I use to keep myself angry about an incident over and done with? Or the ones I use to stop myself from taking a reasonable risk?

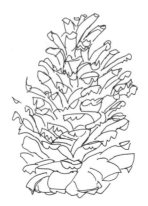

Sometimes fantasies are reminders of unfinished business. Sometimes they are my defense against taking action. Sometimes they are the plea of my organism that I become more aware of a feeling or intuition. Sometimes they are the indirect means I use to criticize myself. Sometimes they are my proposed goals. But fantasies are always *fantasies,* and no matter what the subject, I am fantasizing about myself.

Sometimes if I can look at a dream or fantasy *simply* enough, its meaning becomes clear.

Me: "There is something wrong with my life and I can't figure out what it is."

Dream: "Look, I'll draw you a picture."

What if the world were a dream, and dreams were reality? Now how would I look at everyday life? If I think someone has treated me unfairly, would I react if I knew that person was a figure in a dream?

When I get a clear statement about my life from a dream, it is usually contained more in the emotions than in what I saw. The visual part of the dream often appears to represent what I am feeling during the dream—the individual images taken from situations that have commonly surrounded those emotions. Often they are feelings that I have had recently, especially that day, and they are usually ones I brushed aside. Seen in this way my dreams could be interpreted as saying, "Look what you were feeling today—you didn't fully acknowledge it." Perhaps the fully aware person doesn't dream.

These questions sometimes help me notice something that I wasn't seeing about a dream:

What were my emotions during the dream; what was I feeling or *not* feeling, and how are these emotions familiar?

What was the action of the dream pointing to; what does the action say needs to be done?

Where was the power in the dream; what was controlling?

What was missing in the dream; what would ordinarily be there that was not?

From where or what was a threat coming, and what was the source of blessing?

Did the dream stop short of something happening—
if so, what conclusion do I fantasize?

In what way did the dream say I frustrate myself;
what came in to thwart or change the course of
action?

What was the mood (setting, atmosphere) of the
dream, and how is my life like this?

I believe that dreams serve a useful function within my organism whether I do something with them or not. Most of my dreams don't have a clear, unforced meaning, and if the message doesn't quickly become obvious, I usually drop working on it.

To see more clearly, I merely have to take notice of what can already be seen, rather than looking for what I should be able to see but can't.

We already know enough.

I don't have to *become* aware. I don't have to start
seeing or even learn how to listen. My body is already
aware. I already see. All I need is to be open to my
awareness, to *remain* conscious of what I already
perceive. Awareness is a given and all that is required
is to keep thought out of its way, which of course is
not a doing, but a not-doing.

I hear many people talk about *mindfulness* as if it were
the solution. Mindfulness is a word, a word like *love*,
which has a very roomy definition. But not roomy
enough to include everything.

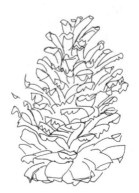

I don't *like* an alarm clock, but it's useful. I don't *like* tension, but it tells me something needs attending. I don't *like* to wince with shame, but it illuminates the dead ends and the side roads.

When Popi Da begins to anticipate our going for a run, he does a series of stretches, yawns, and little squeals. Moosewood and Depot acted exactly the same: as soon as tension started flowing into their muscles they responded by stretching and moving. For all these years I have been reacting to tension by *tightening* my muscles, by freezing them in place, so as not to show it.

Ah, the wisdom of dogs.

My body attempts to look, act, and feel like what I put into it. If in my imagination I hold up all the trash I eat in one hand and hold up my body in the other, what I am doing to myself becomes obvious.

How much tension have I pressed into my body, how much have I strained to keep myself under control? Is it any wonder that I am stiff after compressing myself inside a vice for all these years?

For several months now I have been stretching whatever wants to be stretched, making up how I do it as I go along, letting my muscles and joints tell me what they need, doing it whenever and for as long as it feels good. The effect, especially as compared to routine body-tightening exercises, is so mentally releasing that I believe it somehow nourishes my psyche, just as eating exactly what my system tells me it needs nourishes my flesh.

I think nothing of taking care of my stomach any time of the day that I get hungry. Why not take care of my muscles right when they begin to get tight or tired? And why not befriend my mind when it becomes unfriendly?

This evening I finally did it: I stopped giving myself a headache. When I felt it coming on I stood very still, and let go of all the pushing—and for the rest of the evening my neck and head felt free.

Is my body the mirror of my psyche, and illness but an image?

It seems clear that many of my illnesses have been an externalization of an internal conflict and that my body got sick when I was not letting go.

Allowing the pain to talk to me. *Listening* to the complaints of my body. Noticing what my ulcer forces me to do. Illness is not a spiritual mistake—it is a spiritual reminder.

It is as stupid to judge people for being sick as it is to judge them for receiving guidance.

Tonight when my mother got mad at me, I stood up and stretched my arms toward the ceiling, and when I sat down I found that then I could hear what she saying.

While talking to my landlord this evening I noticed that, as usual, my mouth was open and, as usual, I was swallowing everything he was saying. Once I closed my mouth, I felt less like nodding, more like listening with honesty.

Jan looked up while Rolfing my feet and said that they were sweating heavily. A few days later I noticed that I was only standing on one foot while talking to someone intimidating.

Mike was here when Mother called. After I hung up he told me how he had finally gotten to the point where he could listen to *his* needs while his mother talked to him on the phone.

In what ways do I let people manipulate me? Through politeness? Through threatened anger? Through dangled sex? If someone is mildly abrupt with me, I usually respond in a predictable (controllable) way: I become "a real nice guy."

A healthy response when someone expresses anger, jealousy, or pettiness would be to remember how I was before they expressed it and reclaim that state of mind. To be either offended or obsequious is a form of self-betrayal.

Getting hurt often comes from acting too nice to risk hurting.

Jealousy comes when I fail to use my own power, be my own person, take my own stand. I suspect this is also behind my resentments.

Anger is not power: it is a victim state. When I indulge my anger, I risk damaging myself and destroying a relationship.

To *express* anger is to fail to take responsibility for it.

For too many years I refused to allow myself to acknowledge my anger, which built up in my body and created physical problems. But the answer was not to take the anger out of me and try to give it to someone else. Rather, it was in the recognition that I could both respect the emotion and choose to handle it in a healthy way.

Having finally given myself permission to feel angry, I was able to look at this universally treasured emotion more closely. Why does it, above most other emotions, receive such respect? Because it has the power to induce fear in others? Do I really want to be the kind of person who reacts to every perceived slight by affirming only this one emotion? I think I would rather take several deep breaths and look at the sky, at the trees, at the stars. There is a perceptible smile emanating from Nature.

I suspect that the overfullness of my body is related to the underfullness of my voice: both appear to be ways that I insulate myself from making contact.

Whenever I sit cross-legged my right knee will not go down as far as my left one. This evening, when I was at the play, I noticed that I was holding my right knee up so that it wouldn't touch the person sitting next to me.

Now I see the connection between my leaning over when I walk and my not being open, my not letting people in.

How do I keep people out? What am I doing with my words, my eyes, to keep this person away? Am I letting her voice touch me, or am I only hearing it? Am I using my eyes to see him or to *look* him in the eyes?"

Letting people in is largely a matter of not expending the energy to keep them out.

Sometimes relationships can be so exhausting.

Some of the ways that I have kept myself out of touch with my body:

Consulting a clock to see if I have had enough sleep.
Trying to recall how much I have eaten in order to know how much I want to eat now.
Putting on glasses when my eyes hurt (instead of resting them).
Wearing loose clothes so that I won't feel the objectionable contours of my body.
Putting thick soles and heels between me and the earth.
Breathing through my mouth (which has no sense of smell).
Using strong chemicals to prevent my body from perspiring and having its natural odor.
Never brushing up against a stranger in a crowd.
Holding myself back from touching people when I talk to them.
Not looking at the parts of another person's body that I want to look at.

Another kind of awareness: awareness of the *activity*. Getting into the rhythm of walking. Really *walking*— the whole freely flowing, breathing, swinging, stepping-out, and seeing-it-all-go-by movement. Getting into the rhythm of riding a bike, doing dishes, running, dancing, driving. Awareness of the whole activity that the body is engaged in, as well as awareness of the individual limbs and their motions.

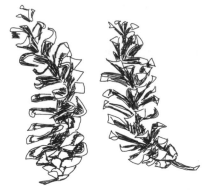

Relaxed muscles do not necessarily make relaxed movements. I have been relaxing my limbs, but my *walk* has remained stiff.

I notice that when I start trying, I literally stick my neck out.

Effortless posture is not holding my body in position but being in position where I am not holding.

As I lay in bed early this morning, too tired to get up but not tired enough to sleep, I thought how typical that moment was of most moments. All the old solutions weren't quite working; there were no apparent new ones, and as usual my latest commandment, "Become aware of how you are doing it," stunk with inadequacy. I spend so much of my time kidding myself that I know something. But there are so few moments when I actually know what is going on, so very, very few.

Every time I think I know something, life keeps on being itself, and I am left standing on my head.

It often seems as if the truth that is helpful today is a lie by tomorrow.

There are no "best ways." There are only alternatives.

One night I had an insight. Afterward I saw the same thing again and again. Then there were other times when I didn't see it, I only said it. If I see something I have never seen before, afterward I am more alert to this new way of looking. But this pattern is not an accumulation of knowledge, because *each time* I have to see it. If the next time I only apply the idea, if I only say the words, then seeing is not going on, only memory is going on, and my organism as a whole is not touched.

I had insights as a Christian Scientist, as an atheist, as a true-believer in Gestalt therapy, as a student of Neuro-Linguistic Programming (NLP), and from many other thought systems. No matter what my premise and no matter what the contradiction, insights followed. The impact of "seeing the light" has sometimes been so intense that it seemed as though I were experiencing a kind of direct perception of reality. But now I doubt that an insight is a revelation. It is probably nothing more than an elaboration of my present standpoint.

The danger with insights is that they are oversimplifications, the attempt to put into words and rules that which is, simply and deeply, best experienced in the moment.

No one thing is more profound than anything else.

Little children use words to have fun, not to "communicate" or "process" or "impress."

Most conversations I hear are carried on as if there really were an answer and as if the people present were actually in possession of it.

I can reverse almost everything I have written and it is equally true.

This turning turning turning of truth
Nothing standing still
And yet the great stillness
and the sameness
The knowing and the never knowing ...

They are towing it in now

But when we talked this morning
of things to be
and my friend sailed out
on the smiling waters

I thought I knew

And when the hallowed old woman said
she loved me

I thought I knew

Then she turned her back
and loosened her bowels
and squatted over my friendship

And years ago when he had forsaken
they nodded his praise

and I nodded too
and thought I knew

Now he is in his bottles of death

And once as I thanked the dear
Lord for my wife and child

I thought I knew

And I turned around
and turned again
and only a wordless house

I thought I knew as
I dove into God's shining Truth
I thought I knew

and now I watch my religions
drop from me like scales

And still the earth keeps turning and
the sun shines on those who know and
refuse to know

Outside my window a bird is singing
The air is still and clear

Recently I have felt very pleasant about my occasional stuttering, and have actually grown fond of my feelings of inadequacy and vulnerability. For the first time in a long while I am beginning to feel quite ordinary and human, and to be very comfortable around other people, just as ordinary and imperfect as me.

Tonight I discovered nature. For the first time I saw it. For the first time I didn't look at it, I listened to it— not with my ears, although I did that too, but with my eyes. Instead of pushing out at it, trying to understand it, I let it speak to me. On my left, some distance away, was the highway. From there I could hear mankind—always arriving, never quite there. Then I looked at the stars. They were silent, and powerful beyond all effort. They were stars being stars and therefore brilliantly alive . . . how puny are words about stars.

"Gorgeous day isn't it?" "Look at the mist over those hills." "Isn't that sunset beautiful?" I wonder why most of us tack a demand for support on every exclamation we make about nature . . . or is it that nature is so boundless that we are always moved to share it?

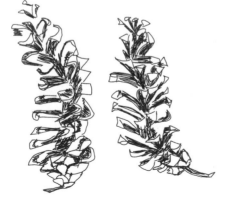

These leaves are not talking about the "autumn of our lives." They are talking about our death. And what a startling speech they deliver: Death can be as useful as life, and even more beautiful.

And here comes the finger
of God,
Strumming down this thread
of mountains,
Bringing seven oceans of
black water
inside a single pillow
of
gray
air

I wish I could take my privacy with me. Solitude
instead of isolation. I am on top of this mesa and still
there are a thousand tongues in my head. Silent
inside, silent and richly alone . . . then there would
be no need to shun.

the absolute stillness of
moonlight
melting
cloud and field and puddle
into
     abstractions
of perfect peace

I believe that at least one of the reasons why prayer, relaxation drills, yoga, self-hypnotism, tai chi, breathing concentration, and mindfulness exercises bring peace and dissolve problems is that they force an end to the merry-go-round of thinking. Either during or after these meditations we do something rare: we stop and listen.

stopping

and counting every sound

stopping

and seeing every stone

stopping

and letting in the wind

stopping

    and not having to be somebody

In order to listen I have to listen without obligation, I have to give up my *intention* to hear. If I will let the meaning flow through me like wind blowing through leaves, then I can open up loosely to what is being said, instead of howling it down with my intensity.

The parent who says, "Now you listen to me!" may be assuring his child's inattention. Recently I have noticed that if I try to concentrate on what someone is saying, I don't hear as well as I can when I broaden my awareness to include more of everything that is going on around me. When I broaden my awareness, the other person's words seem to come more slowly.

I can listen to someone without hearing him. Listening is fixing my attention only on the other person and assuming the posture of attention. Hearing requires that I listen inside me as I listen to him. Hearing is a rhythm whereby I shuttle between the words and my experience. It includes hearing his entire posture: eyes, lips, the tilt of the head, the movement of fingers. It includes hearing the tone of voice and the silences. And hearing also includes attending to my reactions, such as the sinking feeling I get when the other person has stopped hearing *me*.

It's not that I don't listen, it's that I listen to something else. As soon as someone starts talking I immediately start thinking—as if their talking were a waste of my time and now that I have the opportunity to fake it, I will do something that is *really* important.

The difference between talking "at" and talking "with" is the difference between just touching, and touching and being touched.

There are people I meet (very few) whom I feel close to immediately. Agreeableness does not seem to be a factor. There is in fact a decided absence of striving in their manner—they don't *try* to be friendly, they aren't building anything. I also have the feeling that they are very present: they seem more alert to how I am, and what they notice about me appears in their faces fully and instantly. When these people look at me I have the feeling *I* am being seen. They also seem to know what it is they are saying to me, that is, they seem to hear their own words.

It's becoming clear that I see and hear with my entire body. The tension in my stomach and back, the position of my head, the movements of my limbs, all affect the quality of my perception. If my legs are crossed and I open them, if I am leaning intently forward and lean gently back, or if my face is tight and I release the muscles, then a small but measurable change takes place in all the sights and sounds around me.

Last night I was aware that I was using my eyes to signal Jonas Lions. I was having them do a little act entitled, "Jonas, I am very interested in what you are saying." I knew that I was misusing my eyes, but I didn't know how to stop. Maybe if I had started looking at the details of his face and posture to see what *else* he was saying. Or even if I had closed my eyes and noticed how interested I really was. . . . The fear that I am required to *do* something when people talk gets me into this bind.

Maybe this is a richer way to communicate: to respond to how other people are *now* instead of to how they describe themselves; in other words, how they tell me they are, or what they have done or plan to do.

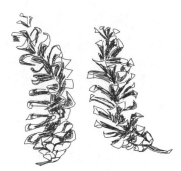

I often get out of balance when I meet someone new, and when René came into the room last night I stopped the light touching of my environment. Maybe next time I will pause to look at all that is going on in the world beside whether or not I am making it with a stranger.

When I meet someone new I evidently see mostly my projections and very little of the person. If my first impressions are negative, they usually turn out to be inaccurate, and if they are positive, they usually turn out to be incomplete.

I seek no imperfections in the piñon and the pine ... and none are seen.

Sometimes when I meet a person I think is superior
to me, I find myself wanting to be their friend.
This kind of desire is neither affection nor respect,
and its very presence hinders the development of a
relationship.

I just discovered that what I thought was my desire
to be friends with Ron was really my desire to appease
the neighborhood bully.

What do I do to keep myself from believing that anyone can like me?

I told Nelson that I agreed with his criticism of one of my books when actually I didn't agree at all. Dishonesty for the sake of appearing honest. What insanity!

Some people are going to like me and some aren't, so I might as well be me. Then at least I will know that the people who like me, like *me*.

I have lost two friends by being open. I once thought that, if I knew anything, I knew that an honest statement of my feelings leads to greater closeness. And sometimes it has. But openness can scare the hell out of people. And there are some who take it as dislike. It has been a relief to realize that I don't have to act the same way around everyone. I can take people as I find them. I can open my eyes and see what effect my words are having, and if my friend is misunderstanding my intentions, I can drop being that way.

Sometimes a particular friendship is simply not worth all the adjustments I have to make in order to maintain it. And sometimes I meet an individual who delights in having enemies and is determined to add me to the list.

A while back I ran into Elbert and was surprised
that he didn't seem excited to see me. Later I realized
that I had never especially liked him either.

I don't really know why people react to me the way
they do. Some end up liking me and some don't, and
in the beginning I seldom know which way it will go.
Nor does there seem to be any need to know.

Likes and dislikes are so frequently mutual that
expecting people to like me when I don't like them is
unrealistic, as well as arrogant.

Beulah cut me off and I am still looking for a nice reasonable explanation for why I hate her guts.

Dislike may at times be a signal similar to pain, and pain means *keep away*, not *destroy*. If I don't like her I don't have to prove her unworthy. The question is not "Is she bad?" but "Is she bad for me?" Or better, "Is she bad for me at this time?"

I suspect that there are many times when I say something critical to a friend, or he does something to annoy me, when our contact has been too prolonged or intense, and one of us is simply feeling the need for a little time off. Now I want to learn how to recognize that need before any words are spoken.

There is an important difference between feeling antagonistic and being critical. When I criticize, in effect I say, "You are wrong," and I leave unspoken my part in the condemnation. Criticism is thus "safer" than acknowledging my feelings as my own—because the other person will respond to the words and not to me. If, however, I say, "This is what goes off in me when you do such and such," I am admitting that all criticism requires a criticizer. But this sounds so phony.

Ninety percent of my problems would be solved if I would just shut up.

So often my confessions are a request for permission: I am testing to see if it will be OK with everyone if I happen to be myself. I tell them what I am like, before I risk being that way.

The effect of flattery is to keep the other person at a distance.

If "guilt is resentment," is adoration a desire for approval?

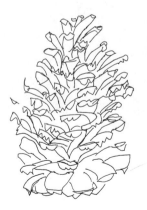

Expressing anger is an intimate act. And so, of course, it is risky. It opens me up to a closer relationship, or to a verbal kick in the groin. I was irritated by Hank's denouncing every comment that anyone made at the meeting, but instead of telling him, I argued against his logic. That was not expressing my irritation, it was reacting to it. Later, when I expressed it directly and told him how mad I was at his attitude, he made a very personal confession of how stupid he felt around all of us. He *could* have come back with a rebuff.

I am surprised at how often my friends seem to appreciate my going to them with my negative feelings. I am afraid that my words will damage our friendship, but they usually strengthen it. This may say more about the quality of my friends than about the wisdom of expressing every negative thought. "Hugh is in his expressing-anger stage, but we will remain his friend anyway."

For seven months I mistook reputation for humanity, politeness for love, being used for being appreciated. For seven months I thought she was my friend . . . and now my hurt and anger at what she has done are making me as petty as she is, and I can't even pretend I am superior.

How can there be pettiness and that sunset on the same planet? Is it possible for me to look at narrowness and cruelty the way I am looking at these clouds? Is there any wonder in the small, selfish parts of mankind? I certainly see none. It's all in this sky.

Gene told me that last night Beulah criticized me in front of several people. Beulah had eaten dinner with us the night before and was very friendly. Why didn't she say those words to me? This situation is classic: One friend tells me what another friend said, and I hurt. I am disappointed in the friend who criticizes, and I question the motives of the friend who reports it. Surely there is a way out of this smallness. How do I make myself ache every time this happens?

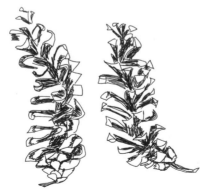

Recently I have been noticing that what I think I want from someone is really what I want from myself. For a long time I have been experiencing Jonas as a know-it-all. Then the other night Gayle said, "Do you realize that you act like a little boy when you're around him?" Of course! What I wanted was not for Jonas to stop being a know-it-all but for me to stop being a know-nothing. (And what I want is not for Lillith to stop being domineering but for me to start standing up for myself.)

If I don't *need* anything from you, I feel freer to tell you what I *want* and to be able to give you what you want.

Other people's traits, if I see them as "faults," tend to draw out the same traits in me. I am controlled by what I experience as "bad" in another person.

Just when I have figured out what I don't like about someone and what I am going to do about it, I will see him again and he will be different.

I don't want to argue any more about how she "is." You see her one way, I see her another way, she sees herself a third way. Now if you want to talk about what how we see her indicates about us....

When I criticize a person, I assume that he has a choice.

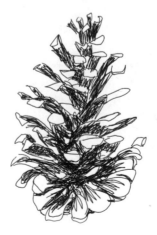

"It's a little thing to do." "You owe her at least that much." "It's your duty." I never realized how powerful is this concept of our owing other people, particularly family. I want to give out of love and respect, not out of fear or duty or some "should" that simply negates any act I might perform because it comes from fear rather than love. The working definition of gratitude is often: "I have done many things for you so now by God you can do this for me." "Do things for" so often translates "give into" rather than "give." If I *give*, that comes from inside.

Kindness: "Will you hurry up dammit—I'm standing here holding the door for you!"

What possible meaning can "I love you" have if it is an answer?

Oh, I see: You want me to do what I want to do whether I want to do it or not.

Kay said, "I want all the gossiping to end now." I felt encumbered. Now I see that Kay was making a resolution, and I see that I don't have to be bound by someone else's resolution—even if she wants me to be.

If I want to make you feel good so that I will feel good, whose interest do I have at heart? If you are feeling bad, will you really be better off if I "make" you feel better?

Last week I realized how often I ask Gayle to do things for me ("While you're up will you ..."). I saw that I wanted to start doing these things for myself, and since I have begun, I have come together in a more comfortable fit.

Gayle always does the laundry, but today when I decided to do it myself I was surprised at my feeling of panic. I see that I have given up more than just drudgery by not doing for myself.

Living without pressure—without putting it on others and without allowing others to put it on me. Living without strings, or selling, or charming, or kidding into compliance, or manipulating through niceness, or threatened anger. Standing in the face of silence, and threats, and expectations, and misunderstandings—standing and *gently* saying, "No thank you, I'll be myself."

Why in the hell am I still trying to reform my dad?

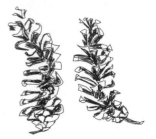

I cannot disregard my relatives in the name of increased awareness. Increased awareness is increased awareness.

I strongly object to the way elderly people are shoved around "for their own good." My grandmother has diabetes, and if knowing this she chooses to eat chocolate, that is her business. I would rather die in one year of candy than in ten of being watched over.

Many self-described "aware" people talk as if a sensual feeling for another is more *legitimate* than a feeling of loyalty for one's spouse. Queen Victoria is simply standing on her head.

"My" son, "my" wife—does the my really bring me closer to them? "Paddlefoot is my horse and I want to take good care of him." But doesn't "my" sooner or later turn into: "Paddlefoot is my horse and I can treat him any way I want?" Which attitude has more potential closeness and consideration: "my child" or, as the Hopis have it, "the child I live with?"

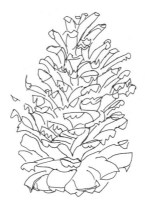

I say "my wife Gayle," Charlotte says "my friend Gayle," Frances says "my daughter Gayle," and *Gayle* remains the same.

Ted "Bull" Howard races his jeep up and down his ranch trying to convince himself that he owns it. Maybe some day he will notice those billion-year-old mountains laughing at him.

I went to my first horse race today and now I want to be rich. "I own it" is the same mental poverty as "I want it." The instant I believe that I own a few things, I exclude myself from all the rest. This strong and periodic wanting begins to recede whenever I remember that everything is mine to enjoy in some way, that anything outside is also inside, and that I live in this earth, and this earth lives in me.

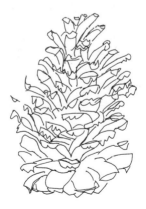

I doubt that any human being can be free of personal beliefs and cherished ideals. I am in less danger of self-delusion if I acknowledge what mine are. I presently have a belief about people that I have no way of testing, and I like believing it. I like how it brings me down when I think I am better, and how it brings me up when I feel less. My belief is that all people have about the same proportion of light and darkness, wisdom and blindness. Only the ways in which we are nourishing or destructive differ, although clearly these differences of expression matter greatly to those on the receiving end. I also have an ideal. It is consideration—not as etiquette, but as a type of awareness that feels good, a sweetly flowing step of connection that follows naturally from the realization that "I am not responsible for you."

I was running in the back hills today, and Anthony came out to ride his bike beside me. To him I was not a "stranger." I was a man running by, and as good a person as any to tell that he hoped very much it would snow in three months.

Why is it that on the highway only children stare out of the rear window and wave at us?

Being habitually silent when a "thank you," a "good-bye," or a "hello" is expected has less integrity than saying these words automatically. The empty form of connection is closer to truth than no connection at all.

My two dogs are hopelessly phony—they are *always*
glad to see me.

In your struggle to be real, to be centered, to be you,
have you left a place for me?

I don't want to do it
but I want to do it for *you*,
so I will do it.

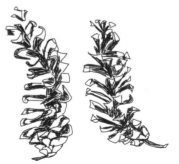

Wanting to do it for you is no less a desire than wanting to do it for me.

I don't want to, but she wants me to—and that counts for something. The question is how much. This question is equally as insistent as "Am I true to myself?" In fact, it is the same.

How deeply am I willing to pierce another human being in order to satisfy my absolute now? I am not responsible for other people, but I can choose to be careful and compassionate. I can choose to be ... and I am knowing right now that I want to.

I could say that if you had been in good shape you wouldn't have hurt when I slugged you in the stomach. I could say that. And I could say that I am not responsible for how you react to my silence or my words. But because I am a human being, I know something about what it is like for you to be human, and this knowledge makes me aware of the probable consequences of my actions.

Today I have seen two people get physically sick from a lack of love while I stood by and did little. I can't force myself to love someone I have no feeling for, but that situation is so rare—what about the ninety-nine percent of the time that I *could* feel love if I would only let go?

Love itself is not an act of will, but sometimes I need the force of my volition to break with my habitual responses and pass along the love already here.

It was Christmas and I wanted to put my arms around
Dad and tell him that I loved him. But I couldn't.
Then it was time to go and I started the drive back. I
hadn't cried about anything for ten years, and I had to
make crying sounds in my throat for almost an hour
before I could start.

A few months ago I was out walking with a friend who is a Gestalt therapist. A man walking from the other direction smiled at us and said, "How are you doing?" My friend didn't answer. He explained to me that the question was phony since the man didn't know us.

Today Nat drove me through the little Spanish villages of northern New Mexico. He waved and shouted greetings out the window and asked directions in self-taught Spanish. He stopped to chat with shopkeepers and spent several minutes of warm conversation with an old drunk. All day his face has been bright with love for these people, and their liking of him has been immediate. Nat is not yet enlightened enough to have reasoned out the impossibility of spontaneous love, and, although he doesn't know it, he has taught me one of the most appreciated lessons of my life.

a willingness
to sway and not
crack
malleable
but not manipulable

a willingness to be
touched
to move off dead center
(but not from my center)
to move and take my center with me
(my strength, my needs, my caring for me)

a willingness to move
to you
and take me
with me

a willingness to see you
to treat you as me
to look from
our eyes with
one vision
to breathe our soul
with one breath

being me
allowing we

it takes such little effort
to reach
out
to another human being

draw a circle around your love
. . . and hate will walk the line

IN THE BEGINNING was the
mist and the dust and the dream.

And I heard a voice walking,
in the cool of the burning,
coming before the fire,
calling to me from the midst
of my awareness saying
Who are you?

And I said I am John.
And he said Who are you?
And I said I am John. And he
said Who are you? And I said:
I AM

Then he closed up the
place of me saying You shall be
One.

AND I JOHN was brought forth
in wisdom and waxed fat and
kicked. And my father filled
my head with soft warm primary
colors and I lived in a
wet dream. For I slept with
the church of my father.

And there appeared in me
a great wonder, and I saw a
new All and a new One. For
last and first were passed
away and there was no more
shore.

And I hid my face in the
image of God and the image
of John was consumed.

And a mighty voice said
Let there be law, and lo,
quiet living law encompassed
and gladdened and constituted
all.

And the law was with God.

And I was one with the law so that the law which was God's was my law and I ruled through all time. Past all space.

And since there was only the law, I the law was all things and I the law was alone. I was everywhere and at once. I did all things at rest.

I the law was God.

BUT IT CAME TO PASS that I saw her coming like the sun rises, for it rose within, a liquid in a liquid a sigh within a sigh.

And her shoulders were licked with starlight and eternity was in her eyes and her hair was soft as angel's breath. But her loins were the howling on high.

And I conceived a love
and bore it, and I John saw
that it was good. And the
love multiplied and subdued
me, for I had never loved
before.

AND BEHOLD a round red
thing lay kindling in the face
of the wilderness. And the
voice closed therein said
Take, eat, this is your body.
 And I took it and ate it
up and my mouth was bitter.
But in my belly it was sweet
as honey. And the voice said
Upon your belly you shall go.
 So I filled my bowels
with the east wind and lifted
the burning lid of hell.
 And I John bred worms
and stank and was like the gods.
 For the smell of fire was
on me.

WHEREFORE I woke. And stood
there with God all over my face.
And night said Wipe him off,
your face comes next.

   For only in your flesh
will you touch flesh and only
with your ears will you hear.
And if your brain offend you
pluck it out.

AND I JOHN came forth and my
eyes were bound with a napkin
and my body was bound with
graveclothes.

And I took from me the
graveclothes and the napkin
and spat on the ground. And
I washed my eyes with the
earth and filled my ears with
the sounds of day.

And the daysounds said
unto the deaf Why reason ye
and why do you remember?
For truth and purpose are night,
and night is death. And death
is a sleep without waking.

AND AFTER TRUTH before all
intendings when now was
forever and here was farther
than space, Man loved.
and his love was light
and light is life
and life lives
eternal
without
dream
ing

About the Author

ugh Prather is the author of eighteen books including the bestselling *Notes to Myself, How to Live in the World and Still Be Happy, Spiritual Notes to Myself,* and *The Little Book of Letting Go.* He lives with Gayle, his wife and co-author of thirty-eight years, in Tucson, Arizona where for many years they were resident ministers at St. Francis in the Foothills United Methodist Church. Hugh is also the host of *The Hugh Prather Show* on Wisdom Radio and Sirius Satellite Radio. Hugh and Gayle have three sons and a dog that thinks she's a cat.

To Our Readers

Conari Press, an imprint of Red Wheel/Weiser, publishes books on topics ranging from spirituality, personal growth, and relationships to women's issues, parenting, and social issues. Our mission is to publish quality books that will make a difference in people's lives—how we feel about ourselves and how we relate to one another. We value integrity, compassion, and receptivity, both in the books we publish and in the way we do business.

Our readers are our most important resource, and we value your input, suggestions, and ideas about what you would like to see published. Please feel free to contact us, to request our latest book catalog, or to be added to our mailing list.

Conari Press
An imprint of Red Wheel/Weiser, LLC
P.O. Box 612
York Beach, ME 03910-0612
www.conari.com